Mexican Cooking for Beginners

How To Prepare Easy Mexican Recipes For Beginners, Enjoy Traditional Mexican Cuisine

ALEXIS MORENO

Sommario

1. SALSA DE AGUACATE (AVOCADO SALSA) 8

2. SALSA DE JITOMATE COCIDA (COOKED TOMATO SAUCE) ... 9

3. SALSA SUPREMA 12

4. SALSA VERDE 13

5. SALSA VERDE 2 15

6. SALSA XCATIC 17

7. SIZZLING STEAKS AND SALSA 20

8. SKINNY MEXICAN-STYLE NACHOS 22

9. SMALL CHICKEN FAJITAS 24

10. SOPAIPILLAS..................................... 26

11. SOPAIPILLAS 2.................................... 28

12. SOUTH OF THE BORDER STEW....................... 32

13. SOUTHWEST BEEF FAJITAS......................... 35

14. SOUTHWEST GUACAMOLE........................... 38

15. SOUTHWEST RIBLETS.............................. 39

16. SOUTHWEST SCRAMBLED EGGS WITH JALAPENO JELLY .. 42

17. SOUTHWESTERN BEEF HASH 44

18. SPANISH RICE 47

19. SPANISH RICE 2 49

20. SPICY MEXICAN TORTILLA STACKS 51

21. SPICY NACHOS SUPREME 53

22. STEPHANIE'S CARNE ASADA 55

23. STUFFED JALAPENOS 57

24. STUFFED MUSHROOMS 58

25. SUPER NACHOS 61

26. TACO CASSEROLE 63

27. TACO CHICKEN WINGS 64

28. TACO MEATBALLS 65

29. TACO PIE 67

30. TEX-MEX BEANS WITH CORNMEAL DUMPLINGS 69

31. TEX-MEX CHILI MEATBALLS WITH ZESTY TOMATO SALSA 72

32.   TEX-MEX HASH.....................................77

33.   TEX-MEX RICE.....................................78

34.   TEX-MEX TORTILLA STACK...........................80

35.   TEX-MEX TUNA SALAD...............................83

36.   TEX-MEX WITH SPINACH BAKE........................85

37.   TEXMEX RED SNAPPER...............................87

38.   THREE BEAN BAKE..................................90

39.   ZUCCHINI RELISH..................................92

40.   ZUNI VEGETABLE STEW..............................94

1. **Salsa De Aguacate (Avocado Salsa)**

3		tomatillos -- husks removed
2	cups	water
2	large	avocados -- peeled and chopped
2		habanero chile -- chopped
3	cloves	garlic
1	small	onion -- chopped

Combine the tomatillos and water and boil until they are soft, about 10 - 12 minutes. Drain and discard the water.

Puree all the ingredients in a blender or food processor, adding a little water if needed to make the salsa smooth and creamy.Serve with tostadas or on a bed of greens for a salad.

2. **Salsa De Jitomate Cocida**

(Cooked Tomato Sauce)

3	Medium	Tomatoes -- broiled
1/4		Onion -- roughly chopped
1	Small Clove	Garlic -- peel & roughly chop
2	Tablespoons	Peanut Oil
1/4	Teaspoon	Salt -- or to taste
tomatoes:		To broil

Many Mexican recipes call for tomatoes to be asodos (roasted). Traditionally they are put onto a hot comal and cooked until the skin is wrinkled and brown and the flesh is soft right through -- this takes about 20 to

25 minutes for an 8-ounce tomato. However, since this method is very messy, it is best to line a shallow metal pan with foil and put the tomatoes in it. Place them under a hot broiler -- do not have the flame too high or the tomato will burn without cooking through

-- and turn them from time to time so that they cook through evenly -- the skin will be blistered and charred. A medium tomato will take about

20 minutes. Blend the tomato, skin, core, and seeds to a fairly smooth sauce. The skin and core give both body and flavor to the sauce. And never mind if the skin is charred: that adds character, too. If

the skin is very badly blackened and hard in places, then remove a little of it. This method of cooking tomatoes makes for a very rich-flavored sauce. Heat the oil, add the blended tomatoes and salt, and cook over a medium flame for about 8 minutes until it has thickened and is well seasoned.

3. **Salsa Suprema**

1	each	Large tomato -- chopped
1	each	Medium onion -- chopped
2	each	Fresh green chilies -- chopped
1	each	Or 4 oz can green chili
1/2	teaspoon	Garlic salt
1/2	teaspoon	Monosodium glutamate (option)
		Salt to taste

Combine all ingredients and chill, covered, in refrigerator at least one hour.

4. **Salsa Verde**

	Garlic cloves
	Scallions
1/2 cup	Parsley leaves
1/4 cup	Cilantro
	Pickled jalapeno pepper
13 ounces	Tomatillos (fresh or canned)
4 ounces	Mild green peppers (chopped)
1/4 teaspoon	Hot pepper sauce
1 teaspoon	Salt (or to taste)

Drop the garlic through the feed tube of a food processor with the metal blade in place and motor running to chop finely (about 10 seconds.) Add the scallions, parsley, cilantro, and jalapeno and chop finely (about 6 pulses   of   the   motor).   Add   the

tomatillos   and   process   until   pureed,

about 5 seconds.Add the remaining

ingredients and pulse

2 times to mix. Refrigerate, covered.

5. **SALSA VERDE 2**

1   can   Mexican   green

tomatoes

(10oz) -- drained

1/4   cup   Onions -- finely chopped

1   tablespoon Cilantro;   coarsely

chopped --

*

1   teaspoon   Canned

Serrano chilis Drained, rinsed --

and Finely chopped

1/4   teaspoon   Garlic -- finely

chopped 1/2 teaspoon Salt

1/8   teaspoon   Freshly   ground   black

pepper

* Also called Chinese Parsley or Fresh

Coriander. In a small bow, combine the

tomatoes, onions, coriander, chili, garlic, salt and pepper to taste. Mix gently, but thoroughly together. Taste for seasoning.

Refrigerate if not to be used immediately. It will only keep for a couple of days. Yield: 1 cup.

6. **Salsa Xcatic**

9		xcatic	-- finely
		chiles *	

chopped

1	medium	white	finely
		onions --	chopped
1/4	cup	vegetable	
		oil	
1/2	teaspoon	salt	
2	tablespoons	white	
		vinegar	

freshly ground black pepper -- to taste

* or substitute yellow wax hot or guero
  chiles.

Yucatan is identified with its native

fiery chile, the Habanero, and the

lesser known chile xcatic, (pronounced

sch-KA-tik). Similar to a chile guero, it is pale green, much hotter, and resembles the New Mexican chile in shape and size.

aute the chiles and onion in the oil for 20 minutes at low heat. Place in a blender with the remaining ingredients and puree until smooth.

Serve over grilled meats, poultry, or seafood.

7. **SIZZLING STEAKS AND SALSA**

3/4 cup   Chopped And Seeded Tomatoes

1/2 cup   Salsa

2 medium   Green   Onions   With   Tops   --

                   Chopped

1/4 teaspoon   Ground Cumin

1/2 cup   Cheddar Cheese -- Finely

                   Cilantro Sprigs

Combine the tomatoes, salsa, onions and cumin and set aside. Trim   the   exterior fat   and   cut   the   boneless   beef   top sirloin   steak   into   4   serving   sized pieces.   Place   each   on   a   flat surface,   cover   with   waxed   paper   and flatten   with   the   bottom   of   a   heavy saucepan, mallet, or cleaver to 1/4-inch thick.   Heat a nonstick frying pan over medium high heat for 2 minutes. Quickly pan broil the steaks for 1 minute.

urn the steaks and top each with an equal amount of cheese. Cook 1 to 2 minutes, DO NOT overcook. Serve the steaks over the

reserved salsa. Garnish with cilantro.

8. **Skinny Mexican-style Nachos**

4oz   low fat tortilla chips

 3/4c   chopped onion

3cloves   garlic -- finely chopped

2tsp   chili powder

1   jalapeno pepper -- finely chopped

 1/2tsp   ground cumin

16 oz   boneless skinless chicken breast --

           cooked/chopped

Preheat oven to 350 degrees. Lay chips
in a 13 x 9 baking pan. Spray large
nonstick skillet with cooking spray.
Heat over medium heat until hot. Add
onion, pepper, garlic, chili powder and
cumin. Cook 5 minutes or until
vegetables are tender, stirring

occasionally. Stir in chicken and tomatoes. Spoon chicken-tomato mixture, cheese, and olives over chips.

Bake 5 minutes until cheese melts. Serve immediately.

9. **SMALL CHICKEN FAJITAS**

1 pound	Chicken Breast -- boneless skinless
	*******Sauce*******
1/2 cup	Soy Sauce
1 cup	Orange Juice
1 tablespoon	Lemon Juice
1 teaspoon	Sugar
2	Cloves Garlic -- crushed
1/2 teaspoon	Ginger
1 tablespoon	Oil
1 medium	Onion -- sliced
1	Green pepper -- sliced
1	Red Pepper -- sliced
12	Flour Tortillas (6-8 inch)

Cut chicken breasts into strips 1/4" thick. Combine all sauce ingredients and pour over chicken strips. Cover and refrigerate overnight. Drain meat well and stir fry in oil along with onion and peppers until all pink color is gone from chicken pieces and vegetables are crisp-tender. Preheat sandwich maker . Trim sides from tortillas to form squares 5 X 5 or 6 X 6 inches.Brush outside of each with oil.Lay 4 tortillas on pocket grid oiled side down. Spoon chicken mixture into the triangle shaped pockets.Top with tortillas, oiled side up. Close lid and cook 3 minutes or until tortillas are heated through and sealed. Repeat with remaining ingredients.Makes 12 pockets.

10. **Sopaipillas**

4	cups	Flour
1	tablespoon	Baking powder
2	teaspoons	Sugar
1 1/2	teaspoons	Salt
1/4	cup	Shortening or lard
1 1/4	cups	Water or more if needed

Sift dry ingredients together. Cut in shortening until crumbly. Add water and mix until holds together. Knead 10-15 times until dough forms a smooth ball. Cover and let set for 20 minutes. Divide dough into two parts.

Roll dough to 1/8" thickness on lightly floured board. Cut into 3" squares or triangles. Do not allow to dry; cover those waiting to fried. When ready to fry, turn upside down so that surface on bottom while resting is on top when frying. Fry in 3" hot oil until golden brown, turning once. Add only a few at a time to maintain proper temperature. Drain on paper towels.

11. Sopaipillas 2

1	package	Active dry yeast
1/4	cup	Warm water (110)
1 1/2	cups	Milk
3	tablespoons	Lard or shortening
1 1/2	teaspoons	Salt
2	tablespoons	Sugar
4	cups	All purpose flour
1	cup	Whole wheat flour
1	each	OIL

In a large mixing bowl, dissolve yeast in warm water. In another bowl combine milk, lard, salt and sugar.

Heat to 110 degrees and add to dissolved yeast. Beat in

3 cups of the all purpose flour and all

of the whole wheat flour. Add abut 1/2

c all purpose flour and mix until a

stiff sticky dough forms. Place dough

on a floured board and knead, adding

more flour as needed, until dough is

smooth and nonsticky.

Place doug in a greased bowl turning

over to grease top. Cover and let stand

at room temp. 1 hour. Punch dough down.

The dough may be covered and chilled as

long as overnight. Knead dough on a

lightly floured board to expel air. Roll

dough out, a portion at a time, to

slightly less than 1/8" thick. Cut in

2"X 5" rectangles or 3" squares for

appetizers. Place on lightly floured

pans and lightly cover. If you work

quickly you can let cut sopaipillas stay at room temp up to 5 min; otherwise, refrigerate them until all are ready to fry. In a deep wide frying pan or kettle heat

1 1/2 - 2 inches oil to 350 on a deep fat frying thermometer. Fry 2 or 3 at a time. When the bread begins to puff, gently push the bread into the hot oil several times to help it puff more evenly. Turn several times and cook just until pale gold on both sides, 1-2 minutes total. Drain on paper towels.

Serve immediately or place in a warm oven until all are fried. Or if made ahead, cool, cover and chill or freeze. To reheat, bake uncovered in a 300 oven, turning once, just until warm, 5-8 min.

Do not overheat or they will become hard.

Makes 2 dozen large sopaipillas or about

4 dozen small ones.

12. SOUTH OF THE BORDER STEW

1/4 cup   Butter

2 pounds   Boneless round steak -- cubed

5   Zucchini -- sliced thin

3 cups   Corn

1 can   (4 oz) grn chilies -- chopped

2   Cloves garlic -- minced

1 teaspoon   Salt

1/4 teaspoon   Oregano

1/4 teaspoon   Cumin

1 cup   Cheddar cheese -- shredded

1/4 cup   Chopped cilantro

In a large skillet, melt butter. Brown

meat, a few pieces at a time. Remove

from skillet as they brown. Saute

zucchini in skillet 7-10 minutes.

Return meat and add corn, chilies,

garlic, salt, oregano and cumin. Simmer, stirring occasionally, about 12-15 minutes or until meat is tender.Stir in cheese until melted.Garnish with chopped cilantro and serve.

13. SOUTHWEST BEEF FAJITAS

		Cucumber Salsa Southwest Relish
		Southwest Guacamole
1	pound	Top Round Steak -- Boneless *
2 1/4	cup	Lime Juice
3	tablespoons	Vegetable Oil
2	teaspoons	Red Chiles -- Ground
2		Cloves Garlic -- Chopped
8		Flour Tortillas **

*   Round Steak should be cut about 1/2 inch thick.

** Flour Tortillas should be 10 inches in Diameter and be warmed.

Prepare Cucumber Salsa, Southwest

Relish, and Southwest Guacamole; set aside. Cut beef steak diagonally across the grain into thin slices, each 2 X 1/8-inch.Mix remaining ingredients except tortillas in a glass or plastic bowl; stir in beef until well coated. Cover and refrigerate for at least

1 hour. Set oven control to broil.Place beef slices on rack in broiler pan. Broil with tops 2 to 3 inches from heat until brown, about 5 minutes. Place 1/8 of the beef, some Cucumber Salsa, Southwest Relish, and Southwest Guacamole in the center of each tortilla.Fold one end of the tortilla up about 1 inch over the beef mixture; fold right and left sides over the folded end overlapping.Fold down

the remaining end. Serve with remaining salsa, relish and guacamole.

14. Southwest Guacamole

5   each   Avocados; Ripe -- Peel & Pit

4   each   Cloves Garlic -- Finely Chopped

1   cup   Tomato; Chopped -- 1 Medium

1/4 cup   Lime Juice

1/2 teaspoon Salt

Mash avocados in a medium bowl until slightly lumpy. Stir in remaining ingredients.Cover and refrigerate 1 hour. Makes 3 cups of dip.

15. **Southwest Riblets**

1/2 cup	Onion; Chopped -- 1 medium
2 tablespoons	Vegetable Oil
1 tablespoon	Red Chiles -- Ground
6 each	Juniper Berries; Dried -- Crush
3 each	Cloves Garlic -- Finely Chopped
1/2 teaspoon	Salt
1/2 ounce	Baking Chocolate -- Grated
1 cup	Water
2 tablespoons	Cider Vinegar
6 ounces	Tomato Paste -- 1 cn.
2 tablespoons	Sugar
3 pounds	Pork Back Ribs; Fresh -- *

* Rack Of ribs should be cut

lengthwise across the bones.

Have the butcher do this with his meat saw.

Cook and stir onion in oil in 2-quart saucepan 2 minutes. Stir in ground red chiles, juniper berries, garlic and salt.Cover and cook 5 minutes, stirring occasionally.Stir in chocolate until melted. Pour water, vinegar and tomato paste into food processor work bowl fitted with steel blade or into a blender container.Add onion mixture and sugar; cover and process until well blended. Heat oven to 375 Degrees F. Cut between pork back ribs to separate.Place in a single layer in roasting pan, pour sauce evenly over pork.Bake uncovered 30 minutes; turn

pork. Bake until done, about

30 minutes longer.

16. Southwest Scrambled Eggs with Jalapeno Jelly

1/2		onion
3	tablespoons	margarine
6		eggs
2	tablespoons	jalapeno jelly -- * see note
3	ounces	cream cheese

* See recipe in this cookbook to make your own Jalapeno Jelly, or you can use a store-bought one for this recipe. A food processor is not necessary for the preparation of this recipe, but it will take longer without.

Fit the steel knife blade into the work bowl of the food processor. Process onion until chopped in 1/4-inch pieces.

42

Melt margarine in a medium skillet.

Saute onion in skillet until tender.

With steel knife blade still attached,

process eggs, jelly and cream cheese

until smooth, about 30 seconds. Pour

mixture into skillet with onions and

scramble until eggs are dry.

Serving Ideas : A special breakfast or brunch

dish.

NOTES : Serve with plenty of fresh

fruit, homemade muffins, sausage or

ham and coffee.

17. Southwestern Beef Hash

1	Lb	Lean Ground Beef
1	Sm	Onion -- chopped
3	C	Frozen Potatoes Obrien
1/2	Tsp	Salt
1/4	Tsp	Pepper
1	C	Salsa
		Sliced Green Onions -- optional
		Sliced Black Olives -- optional

Brown ground beef and onion in large skillet over medium heat until no lnger pink.

Drain. Stir in potatoes, salt, and pepper. Increase

heat to medium-high and cook 5 minutes, stirring occasionally.Stir in salsa. Cook 8 to 10 minutes more until potatoes are lightly browned, stirring occasionally. Garnish with green onions and black olives, if desired.

Yield: 4 servings.

18. **Spanish Rice**

3	tablespoons	Shortening
1 1/2	cups	Rice
1/2	cup	Onion -- sliced
1/2	cup	Bell pepper -- sliced
1	each	14 oz can whole tomatoes
1	each	Medium clove garlic -- minced
1	teaspoon	Black pepper
2	teaspoons	Salt
3	cups	Water

Melt shortening in large skillet. Add rice and brown. When rice is a golden brown, reduce heat and add onion, bell pepper, tomatoes, garlic and pepper. Mix well and add 1 1/2 cups warm water or enough to just cover the rice. Add salt.

Cover and let simmer until almost dry.

Add remaining water, cold, a little at a

time, cooking over low heat until

fluffy. Note: You may substitute peeled

seeded green chili for the bell pepper.

19. **Spanish Rice 2**

1	cup	Uncooked long grain rice
4	tablespoons	Oil
2	tablespoons	Diced bell pepper
3	tablespoons	Diced onion
1	teaspoon	Dried parsley flakes
3	ounces	Tomato paste
2	each	Cloves garlic -- minced
2	cups	Cold water
1/2		
3/4	teaspoon	Salt

Lightly brown rice in oil over medium heat, stirring constantly. Add bell pepper and onion and saute' five minutes more, stirring often. Remove from heat; add parsley, tomato paste and garlic.

Stir well and then add water and salt.

Heat mixture to boiling, cover tightly

and simmer 20 to 30 minutes or until

liquid is absorbed. Remove from heat and

let steam 10 minutes before serving.

20. SPICY MEXICAN TORTILLA STACKS

1	can	Pinto Beans (15oz), drained -- rinsed
1	can	Black Beans (15oz), drained -- rinsed
1	can	Corn (16oz)
1	can	Chopped Green Chilies (4oz)
1	large	Onion -- chopped
1	large	Green Pepper -- chopped
5		Flour Tortillas
1	cup	Monterey Cheese -- pre-shredded
1	cup	Cheddar Cheese -- pre-shredded
1	large	Jar Salsa

Preheat oven 425". Combine beans and corn in large bowl. Stir in chilies, onion and green pepper. Lay one tortilla at the bottom of a greased two-quart souffle or casserole dish. Spoon a small amount of bean mixture over tortilla. Top with equal amounts of Moterey Jack and cheddar cheese. Continue alternating layers of tortilla, bean mixture and cheese mixture until you end with cheese layer. Bake covered at 425" for 10 minutes. Serve with salsa.

21. **Spicy Nachos Supreme**

8ounces	Tomato Sauce
4ounces	Diced Green Chiles
1/2 cup	Chopped Green Bell Pepper
1	Green Onion -- Sliced
1/4 teaspoon	Hot Pepper Sauce
10 ounces	Tortilla Chips
2 cups	Shredded Cheddar Cheese
1	Avocado
1 teaspoon	Lemon Juice
1/2 cup	Sour Cream
	Jalapeno Slices -- Optional

Combine tomato sauce, chiles, green pepper, green onion and hot pepper sauce in a bowl; let stand for 15 minutes.

Place tortilla chips in

a shallow 8" X 10" baking dish. Pour sauce over chips; sprinkle grated cheese over all.   Broil   nachos   for   3 minutes or until cheese melts.

Just before serving, seed, peel and mash avocado.Stir in lemon juice. Spoon avocado mixture and sour cream on hot nachos and top with jalapeno slices. Serve immediately.

22. STEPHANIE'S CARNE ASADA

1		20 oz top sirloin steak
2	tablespoons	Vegetable oil
1/2	teaspoon	Dried leaf oregano - crushed
1/2	teaspoon	Salt
1/4	teaspoon	Coarsely ground pepper
1/4	cup	Orange juice
1	tablespoon	Lime juice
2	teaspoons	Cider vinegar
2		Orange slices -- 1/2" thick

Place steak in a shallow glass baking dish. Rub with oil on each side. Sprinkle with oregano, salt and pepper. Sprinkle orange juice, lime juice, and vinegar over the steak. Cover and refrigerate overnight for best flavor or several hours, turning occasionally.

To cook, bring meat to room temperature. Prepare and preheat charcoal grill (or gas grill). Drain meat, reserving marinade. Place steak on grill. Top with orange slices. Occasionally spoon reserved marinade over steaks as they cook. Grill 3-4 minutes on each side, or until medium-rare. Cook longer if desired. Remove orange slices to turn steak. Replace orange slices on top of steak.

23. STUFFED JALAPENOS

24	Jalapenos -- halved & de-veined
6 1/2 Ounces	Tuna, water pack -- drained
1/2 Cup	Pecans -- finely chopped
	Mayonnaise

Mrs. Tom Dudley

Comanche (TX) Garden Club Cookbook

1967

Halve and de-vein jalapenos. In a bowl, mix tuna and pecans with enough mayonnaise to moisten. Stuff jalapeno halves.

24.**Stuffed Mushrooms**

24 each   Mushrooms -- Medium

2   tablespoons Margarine Or Butter

1/4 cup   Onion; Chopped -- 1 Medium

2   tablespoons White Wine -- Dry

1/4 cup   Bread Crumbs -- Dry

1/4 cup   Cooked Smoked Ham -- Fine Chop

2   tablespoons Parsley -- Snipped

1   tablespoon Lime Juice

1   each   Clove Garlic -- Finely Chopped

1   teaspoon   Oregano Leaves -- Dried

                 Dash Of Pepper

1/2 cup   Cheese; Finely Shredded -- *

*   Use Monterey Jack Cheese in this recipe.

Cut stems from mushrooms; finely chop

enough stems to measure 1/4 cup. Heat

margarine in 10-inch skillet just until

bubbly. Place mushroom caps, topsides down, in margarine. Cook uncovered until mushrooms are light brown; remove mushrooms with slotted spoon. Cook and stir onion in same skillet until tender; stir in wine. Simmer uncovered 2 minutes. Mix in chopped mushroom stems and remaining ingredients except cheese and mushroom caps; cool slightly. Shape mixture into 24 small balls; place 1 in each mushroom cap.Sprinkle with cheese.Set oven control to broil. Place mushroom caps on rack in broiler pan. Broil with tops 3 to 4 inches from heat until cheese is melted, about 3 minutes.

25. **Super Nachos**

1	can	refried beans
1	can	green chilis
2	cups	monterey jack cheese
2	cups	cheddar cheese -- (velveta best)
3/4	cup	taco sauce
1/2	cup	sliced black olives -- or to taste
1	tsp	lemon juice
1	cup	sour cream
		tortilla or nacho chips

Brown ground beef, add onion and cook

until tender. Drain fat, add

salt and pepper to taste.

Spread refried beans in a 10"x13" baking

dish.Top with meat. Place green chilis on top.Mix monterey jack and cheddar cheese together and sprinkle on top. Drizzle taco sauce over evenly and bake uncovered 20-25 minutes 400 degrees.Remove from oven. Mix black olive with lemon juice and spread them on top.Cover with sour cream and serve at once with chips.

26. TACO CASSEROLE

1	pound	Hamburger
1		Envelope taco seasoning mix
1	can	Tomato sauce
1	cups	Water
1/2		
1	cup	Grated cheese (more if you -- want it)

bag baked tortilla chips

Saute meat in skillet. Add taco seasoning mix, tomato sauce, and water. Bring to a boil, reduce heat, and simmer uncovered 15 min. Add tortilla chips; mix, being careful not to break the chips. Pour into a 2-inch- deep by 8 inch round or square baking dish. Bake in 400 oven 10-15 minutes. Top with

27. Taco Chicken Wings

2 1/2 pounds   Chicken Wings

1   Envelope Taco Seasoning Mix *

2   cups   Dry Bread Crumbs

1   Jar (16oz) Taco Sauce **

* 1-1/4 oz Old El Paso ** Old El Paso

Remove wing tips and discard. Cut wings at joint. Combine bread crumbs and taco seasoning mix; mix well. Preheat oven to 375. Dip each chicken piece in taco sauce then roll in bread crumbs; coat thoroughly. Place on lightly greased baking sheet.

Bake for 30-35 mins.

28.**Taco Meatballs**

1 pound	Beef -- ground
1 cup	Green pepper
1 cup	Rice -- cooked
2 teaspoons	Garlic salt
11ounces	Cheddar cheese soup
1 cup	Onion
1 cup	Celery
2 each	Egg -- beaten
8 ounces	Taco sauce

Mix all but last two ingredients. (I puree vegetables in blender rather than chopping.) Form meat balls and place in 2- 1/2 qt. dish.Bake at 350 degrees for 30 minutes. While baking, heat taco sauce and soup on stove. Pour over meatballs and bake another

29. **Taco Pie**

1	package	Crescent rolls
1	package	Taco mix
2	cups	Corn chips -- crushed
1	cup	Cheddar -- shredded
1	pound	Hamburger
1/2	cup	Water
1	cup	Sour cream

Cook hamburger, taco mix and water according to package directions. Place unrolled crescent dough in ungreased pie plate to form crust.

Sprinkle with half of the corn chips and top with hamburger mixture.

Spread sour cream on top and cover with cheese and remaining chips. Bake at 375 degrees for 20 minutes or until heated

through.

30. TEX-MEX BEANS WITH CORNMEAL DUMPLINGS

1/3 cup	Flour
1 teaspoon	Baking powder
	Beaten Egg White
2 tablespoons	Cooking Oil
1 cup	Chopped Onion
15 ounces	Can Garbanzo Beans -- drained
15 ounces	Can Tomato Sauce
2 teaspoons	Chili powder
1 1/2 teaspoons	Cornstarch
1/3 cup	Yellow Cornmeal
1/4 teaspoon	Salt
1/4 cup	Skim Milk
3/4 cup	Water
	Clove Garlic -- minced

15   ounces   Can Red Kidney Beans   --
             drained

4   ounces   Can diced green chili pepper

  1/4 teaspoon   Salt

In a med mixing bowl, stir together
flour, cornmeal, baking powder, and
1/4 t salt; set aside. In a small bowl
combine egg white, milk, and oil; set
aside.

In a 10" skillet combine the water,
onion, and garlic. Bring to boiling;
reduce heat. Cover and simmer 5 minutes
or till tender. Stir in garbanzo beans,
kidney beans, tomato sauce, drained green
chili peppers, chili powder, and 1/4 t
salt.

In a small bowl stir together cornstarch

and 1 T water. Stir into bean mixture.

Cook and stir till slightly thickened and

bubbly. Reduce heat. For dumplings, add

milk mixture to cornmeal mixture; stir

just until combined. Drop dumpling

mixture from a Tablespoon to make 5

mounds atop bean mixture.

Cover and simmer for 10-12 minutes or till

a toothpick inserted in the center of a

dumpling comes out clean.

31. Tex-Mex Chili Meatballs with Zesty Tomato Salsa

3	tablespoons	Vegetable oil
1	small	Onion, diced -- about 1/2 cup
	1/2 teaspoon	Chili powder
1	pound	Lean ground beef
1	large	Egg
1	can	(4 oz) mild green chilies Drained and chopped
	1 3/4 cups	Fresh bread crumbs -- about 4 Slices bread
	1/3 cup	Shredded Monterey Jack Cheese
	1/3 cup	Shredded mild Cheddar

		Cheese
3/4 teaspoon		Salt
6		Corn tortillas -- half 10 oz.
		Pkg. -- cut into wedges
1		Zesty Tomato Salsa
		Lettuce leaves -- optional
		Tomato wedges -- optional

-----ZESTY TOMATO SALSA-----

1	tablespoon	Vegetable oil
1		Red pepper, cored -- seeded
		And diced (about 2 cups)
1		Green bell pepper, cored
		Seeded and diced (about 2 Cups)

1	medium	Onion -- diced (about 3/4 cup
1	large	Clove garlic -- crushed
2	large	Ripe tomatoes -- diced (about
2		cups)
	1/2 teaspoon	Hot red pepper sauce

Heat the oven to 400 degrees. In 12" skillet,over medium high heat, heat 1 tbsp.vegetable oil;add onion and chili powder;cook about 10 minutes,stirring frequently,until onion is tender and coated with chili powder. Remove onion to large bowl;wipe skillet clean. To bowl with onion,add beef,egg,chilies,bread crumbs,1 tbsp. of each of cheeses and salt;using hands or wooden spoon,blend well. Shape mixture into 1 1/4" balls. In skillet over medium-high heat,heat remaining 2 tbsp. oil;add meat mixture;cook 15 minutes,turning frequently,until well browned on all sides and cooked through. Meanwhile,place tortilla chips in single layer

on jelly-roll pan;bake 10 minutes until crisp and golden. Prepare Zesty Tomato Salsa. To serve:Spoon meatballs into center of large serving platter;sprinkle with remaining Monterey Jack and Cheddar cheese.

Arrange tomato wedges and lettuce around meatballs if desired. Serve with tortilla chips and salsa. Makes 4 servings. ZESTY TOMATO SALSA: In a 2 qt. saucepan over medium high heat, heat 1 tbsp. vegetable oil; add 1 each red and green bell pepper, cored, seeded and diced (about 2 cups), 1 medium size onion, diced (about 3/4 cup) and 1 large clove garlic, crushed. Cook about 10 minutes, stirring frequently, until tender. Stir in 2 large fresh, ripe tomatoes, diced (about 2 cups) and 1/4 to 1/2 tsp. hot red pepper sauce; cook 1 minute longer until heated through. Makes about 1 1/2 cups.

32. **TEX-MEX Hash**

1pound   Ground beef

1each   Green pepper -- chopped

 1/2 cup Rice -- uncooked

2teaspoonsSalt

3each   Onion -- sliced

1can   Tomato -- whole (medium can)

1teaspoon Chili powder

           Pepper -- dash

Preheat oven to 350 degrees. Pan fry ground beef until light brown in skillet. Drain fat. Add onions & peppers and cook until onion is tender. Stir in rest of ingredients and heat until warm. Pour in a casserole dish, cover, bake for 1 hour.

33. TEX-MEX RICE

3/4 cup		Onion -- chopped
2	tablespoons	Olive Oil
1	cup	Rice -- raw
1/4 teaspoon		Black Pepper
2		Garlic Cloves
2 1/2 cups		Vegetable Broth
1 1/2 teaspoons		Ground Cumin
1		Red Bell Pepper

Mince garlic. Remove seeds and dice bell pepper.

In dutch oven, cook onion, garlic and raw rice in oil until onion is tender and rice is lightly browned.

Add chicken broth and bring to a boil.

Stir in cumin and black pepper. Cover tightly and simmer 20 minutes. Remove

from heat. Stir in bell pepper.Let
stand covered until all liquid is
absorbed, about 5 minutes.

34. TEX-MEX TORTILLA STACK

1	9-oz. pkg. (2 cups) frozen
	Chopped cooked chicken
1 cup	Finely chopped -- peeled
	Jicama
1/2 cup	Taco sauce
8	10-inch flour tortillas
1	6-oz. container frozen
	Avocado dip -- thawed
2 cups	Chopped lettuce
1	16-oz. can refried beans
	With green chili peppers or
	Mexican-style beans -- drained
	And mashed
1	8-oz. carton reduced-fat or
	Regular dairy sour cream

1/2 cup   Chopped red sweet pepper

1/3 cup   Sliced green onion

1 cup   Shredded lower-fat or

            Regular cheddar cheese -- or

            Monterey Jack cheese with

            Jalapeno peppers

1/4 cup   Sliced pitted ripe olives

            Taco sauce (optional)

THAW CHICKEN: In a medium mixing bowl combine chicken, jicama, and the 1/2 cup taco sauce; set aside.

PLACE ONE OF THE FLOUR TORTILLAS on a platter.   Spread w: spread with half of the beans. Top with another tortilla; add half each of the sour cream, red pepper, green onion and cheese.

REPEAT LAYERS, ending with remaining sour cream, red pepper, green onion, and cheese.Sprinkle with olives. Serve right away or cover and chill for up to 3 hours.TO SERVE, cut into wedges. Pass taco sauce. Makes 8 main-dish servings.

35. TEX-MEX TUNA SALAD

2	cans	Solid white tuna in water -- drained and flaked
1/2	cup	Sliced ripe olives
1/2	cup	Sliced green onions w/tops
1/2	cup	Thinly sliced celery
2/3	cup	Pace Picante Sauce
1/2	cup	Dairy sour cream
1	teaspoon	Ground cumin
		Lettuce leaves -- OR Shredded lettuce
12		Taco shells -- OR
3	cups	Tortilla chips

Combine tuna, olives, green onions and celery in medium bowl. Combine Pace Picante Sauce, sour cream and cumin; mix well. Pour over tuna mixture; toss

83

lightly. To serve, line taco shells with lettuce leaves; spoon tuna mixture into shells. Or, line individual serving plates with shredded lettuce; top with tuna mixture and surround with tortilla chips.

Drizzle with additional Pace Picante Sauce; top with additional sour cream, if desired.

36. **TEX-MEX WITH SPINACH BAKE**

2	cups	Bisquick baking mix
	1/2 cup	Water -- cold
1	pound	Ground beef
1	package	Taco seasoning mix
1	cup	Water
10	ounces	Spinach *
1	cup	Cheese -- ricotta
	1/3 cup	Green onions -- chopped
1	1/2 cups	Cheddar cheese -- shredded
1	cup	Sour cream
1		Egg -- lightly beaten

* frozen, thawed, chopped and squeezed dry.

Heat oven to 350~F. Combine baking mix

and 1/2 c cold water; stir until soft

dough forms.

Press dough into bottom of greased 13x9" baking

dish.

Cook ground beef in large nonstick skillet until brown. Stir in taco seasoning mix (dry) and 1 c water.

Bring to a boil; reduce heat and simmer 15 minutes, stirring occasionally.

Spoon mixture over dough.

Combine spinach, ricotta cheese and onions; spread over ground beef mixture.

Combine Cheddar cheese, sour cream and egg; spoon evenly over spinach mixture. Bake 30 minutes or until set. Let stand 5 minutes before serving.

37. TEXMEX RED SNAPPER

2	tablespoons	Olive or salad oil
1		Large onion -- chopped
2		Cloves garlic -- minced
4	teaspoons	Sugar
1	teaspoon	Salt
1/4	teaspoon	Cinnamon -- ground
1/4	teaspoon	Cloves -- ground
5	cups	Peeled, seeded -- chopped tomato
1 1/2	teaspoons	Each: water & lemon juice
1	tablespoon	Cornstarch
2		Jalapenos, seeded -- chopped
2	tablespoons	Capers
5 1/2	pounds	Red Snapper, cleaned,

scaled

Head removed

1/3 cup   Pimento   stuffed   green

olives

Sliced thin.

3   tablespoons Chopped fresh cilantro

Heat oil in wide frying pan over med heat; add onion and garlic and cook, stirring often, until onion is soft.tir in sugar, salt,cinnamon, cloves, and tomatoes.ook, stirring, over high heat until a thick sauce forms (abt. 8 min.). Blend together lemon juice, water, and cornstarch; stir into tomato mixture.Cook until mixture boils and turns clear; remove from heat. Stir in chiles and capers. Rinse fish, pat dry.

Place a 24 inch sheet of foil crosswise in a large roasting pan. Grease foil lightly (spray with Pam), then place fish on foil; pour hot tomato sauce over fish. Bake, uncovered, in a 400 F. oven until fish flakes when prodded with fork inthickest part (abt. 45 min). Baste frequently with sauce during last 15 min. of baking.Skim watery juices off sauce with a spoon; then stir sauce to blend. Lift foil, fish , and clinging sauce and slide onto a platter; drizzle with remaining sauce in pan. Garninsh with olives and cilantro. To serve, cut fish to bone, then lift off each serving.

38. THREE BEAN BAKE

16ounces	Can Great Northern Beans -- undrained
16ounces	Can Chili beans -- undrained
in	Mexican section -- of store)
16ounces	Can Kidney Beans -- drained
1/3 cup	Ketchup
1/3 cup	Firmly packed brown sugar
1/2	Powered ginger
	teaspoon

In 2 quart microwave safe casserole or dish, combine all ingredients. Mix well.   Cover with Waxed Paper. Microwave on HIGH for 8 - 11 minutes, stirring twice during cooking. If thicker juice is wanted,

Micro in two min increments on 80% power. Stir often.

CROCK POT Directions. Combine all ingredients, mix well. Cover - cook on High setting for 2 hours. If thicker juice is wanted, remove cover, cook 1 hour longer, stirring occasionally.

39. Zucchini Relish

2	cups	Zucchini -- Shredded
1/4	cup	Fresh Cilantro -- Snipped
2	tablespoons	Lime Juice
2	tablespoons	Vegetable Or Olive Oil
1	teaspoon	Salt
1/4	teaspoon	Sugar
1/4	teaspoon	Pepper

Mix all ingredients in glass or plastic bowl.Cover and refrigerate at least 1 hour. Makes about 1 1/4 cups relish.

40. Zuni Vegetable Stew

3/4	cup	Onion -- Chopped
1	each	Clove Garlic -- Finely Chopped
2	tablespoons	Vegetable Oil
1	each	Red Bell Pepper; Large -- *
2	each	Chiles; Medium Size -- **
1	each	Jalapeno Chile -- Seed & Chop
1	cup	Squash -- Cubed ***
29	ounces	Chicken Broth -- 2 cans
1/2	teaspoon	Salt
1/2	teaspoon	Pepper
1/2	teaspoon	Coriander -- Ground
1	cup	Zucchini -- Thinly Sliced
1	cup	Yellow Squash -- Thinly Sliced
17	ounces	Whole Kernel Corn -- Drained
16	ounces	Pinto Beans; Drained -- 1 can

Bell pepper should be seeded and cut into

2 X 1/4-inch strips. ** Chiles should be either poblano or Anaheim and should be seeded and *** Use either hubbard or acorn squash. (about 1/2 pound)

Cook and stir onion and garlic in oil in 4-quart Dutch oven over medium heat until onion is tender. Stir in bell pepper, poblano and jalapeno chiles. Cook for 15 minutes. Stir in Hubbard squash, broth, salt, pepper and coriander. Heat to boiling; reduce heat. Cover and simmer until squash is tender, aobut 15 minutes. Stir in remaining ingredients. Cook uncovered, stirring occasionally, until zucchini is tender, about 10 minutes.

CPSIA information can be obtained
at www.ICGtesting.com
Printed in the USA
BVHW041350200421
605393BV00001B/101